RAMBLINGS of A BLETHER

Kirsteen M Murray

ISBN: 978-1-912270-60-6

First published in 2019 by
For The Right Reasons
(Charity no. SC037781)
Printers & Publishers
38-40 Grant Street, Inverness

British Library Cataloguing in Publication Data.
A catalogue record of this book is available
from the British Library.

Contents

WHEN HOLLYWOOD BECKONS

You, my friends, have been incredibly supportive during this process of what essentially is crowd funding and me sorting out my Christmas presents for this year. Particularly those of you who have trawled through the offerings, even the ones that have not eventually made the cut. And many many thanks to the lovely Emma Pirrie for the artwork on the cover.

The talk eventually meanders into the realms of fantasy. The commonest is who will play me in the Hollywood movie. This is sheer lunacy. The best and the brightest stars of stage and screen have been considered in our discussions. The majority have reluctantly been discarded on the grounds they are just too old. There is nothing like a Dame, but by the time the finance is put in place, and even with the best in Photoshopping, the moment will have been lost. The most favoured contender has ended up being Mrs Brown. A fine figure of a woman, with the necessary presence.

Another school of thought has advocated cartoon caricature type presentation. This has merit. You can pick a shape and face, and generally have a lot of fun. But who will do the voice? I could do it myself, but would alienate the audience, a lot of folk being unable to follow and understand an Islander, but even more folk requiring a retuning. Those folk, of course, are more to be pitied than censured.

But, really, this isn't about a best seller. I have been very clear from the start that I do not expect or anticipate any such thing. Can I be bothered being famous? No. I do not want to have to think about what I am wearing before I go to the Co-op and worry if my hair is brushed. Paparazzi at the door. Friends and family being quizzed about my back story.

So, phew, this is at least one worry off my mind. The likelihood of any such thing as an imminent trip to Hollywood is remote to non-existent. But thank you for the chortles we have had as we have considered it. Great fun and nonsense. It is enough that you have put your hand in your hipper and taken out the necessary to purchase the ramblings of a blether. Thank you from the bottom of my heart. Enjoy.

THE MOST BORING MAN

This is a controversial title, I know. The competition has been fierce, but the winner is worthy, and eventually led the field to romp home. I can remember him vividly. Which is extremely annoying, as I have only vague memories of conversations with interesting men; only a warm glow of remembered laughter.

As I entered the lift on that fateful day, Otis was the sole occupant. First impressions were fairly bland. Just an ordinary individual, suited and booted, and generally looking like a Lance Corporal of British industry. Of course, there is an etiquette to being in a lift. You can't stare, and indeed eye contact is best avoided. You are in a confined space with someone you have not been introduced to. It is unnecessary to initiate conversation. You are going from A to B in a vertical direction, at speed, and it is safe to assume that you will continue the rest of your life without their input.

That's the normal course of events. But (and here is the rub) the blessed lift broke down, in between floors. Now the lifts in this day and age have phones, and instructions on what to do in the event of a malfunction. But transplant yourself back to the early 80's and pre mobile phones, and you get the picture. It was an impressive shuddering stop.

Now I dislike heights. This wasn't one of those lifts with a glass floor – ridiculous idea. But a film had been released around about this time, involving broken cables, and lifts plunging, mass death and chaos ensued. This dreadful thought flashed through my psyche. Aaaargh.

It was at this point that Otis decided to introduce himself and take charge of the situation. His name wasn't Otis, but he was a lift salesman. His patter started with an explanation that if his firm had built this particular lift, the chances of it breaking down would have been negligible. Their lifts never broke down, while this shoddy, poorly designed excuse for a lift was obviously not fit for purpose. He then caused my heart to lurch against my rib cage as he proceeded to jump up and down in an effort to jump start the lift. I was beginning to feel that much more of this and he would get an ear adjusted with a side swipe from my handbag. A feeling of dislike for him was growing apace.

We had no way of knowing if anyone else had realised the lift had broken down. I was now worried that the lift would run out of oxygen, and I was going to be entombed with Otis. However, before I started screaming for help - I didn't want to waste oxygen - I tried to be rational. It was 3pm, and the lift was in a busy office block. It was surely reasonable to suspect that lazy people, who avoided stairs, would notice the failure of the light indicating which floor the lift was on, would raise the alarm, and rescue me.

Otis had not been idle while I was thinking those dark thoughts. In fact he had not stopped talking since the lift had stilled. His voice was clipped and nasal, with a high squeaky tone. Annoying, that's what I am driving at. My last nerve ending was getting grated by the sheer inanity of his prattling. He appeared to be reciting the trade catalogue of his firm's lifts. Comparing the A334r5f model with the more recently upgraded B443r5f model. How he thought this would be of any interest to me, I cannot imagine. In short the subject matter failed to grip.

Of course he had his own cross to bear. He was after all stuck in a lift with me. I am sure he was not delighted either at being stuck, or the company he was lumbered with. And no doubt the way I was ignoring him as best I could, hurt the ego. I was not responding, in any way, to the wearisome prattle. Mind you, I say that, but I no doubt gave him 'one of my looks.' Those looks, I am led to understand by those who have been scorched by them, have a fairly decent chance of stopping a rhino mid charge. I obviously wouldn't consider conducting an experiment with an endangered beast just to check out the force of their argument, but subliminally, I may have made my displeasure with the bloke evident. Who can say? Passage of time and all that. Also, once we left the lift, I had no intention of ever seeing him again, far less conduct an exit interview. Who knows what lies ahead of us in life, if I had suspected that I was going to make him a star in one of my ramblings I might have shown more interest. In fact any interest. The bar as far as Otis was concerned was barely off terra firma.

Three hours, my friends. Three hours in that lift. When the doors opened and rescue occurred I didn't know what to do first – light up a ciggie, kiss the floor or go to the toilet. A tumult of emotion. That's what I'm talking about.

But you know, I owe that man Otis an immeasurable debt of gratitude. He has set the bar for the last thirty-five years for me. Now when I find my mind wandering, running away from the present, perhaps because I am confronted with someone or something I dismiss initially as boring, I think no. In comparison to Otis, this is possibly interesting. Of course it doesn't always work. And another contender in the most boring man competition is lead up to the starting line, the man who spoke about widgets being the latest in a long line.

I can hear you wonder dear reader, for the sake of political correctness, perhaps the next ramble should be about the most boring woman? But no. These are my rambles, and I ramble and meander like a mountain stream. You have heard the last of my blethers on boring. I am bored of the subject now, and will desist.

ROOM 240

Bags packed, dog fostered, excitement mounting, I finally place my bum on a train seat. Ah! The planning for 'D' day has been worth it. I'm heading from the Highlands to Newcastle to see my 3 sons who are at various stages of study, and I can't wait. It must be over fifteen years since I went on a jaunt by myself. And to go by train! I always feel I'm going somewhere on a train. Ferry boat travel is ten a penny, but not a train. That's special to me.

The journey was blessedly uneventful. I was so chilled I didn't even quibble at the exorbitant price of coffee. I cared not one jot.

Arriving I struggled with bags over bridge to exit. Couldn't work out how to put ticket in machine in a way that either it or me could allow me to get through. With the help of a reluctant attendant – not as homely or nice as in Inverness – the paddle was soon patting me on the bum, through to Newcastle.

A joyous welcome awaited. Not immediately though, my eldest was twenty the previous day, and was limping slowly to the station, having been plucked from the dreamless half an hour prior. I had passed number two son, in a blur of excitement, intent on restoring nicotine levels after the five and a half hour journey. I'd been threatening to wear my high-vis red shawl down, and my incognito brown leather jacket had not caught his eye. After repairing to the Irish hostelry across the road, the meeting was complete when number three son arrived.

The first night was spent in a student flat. What really swung the hotel as opposed to the deluxe student flat was the complete absence of hot water.

Entering the Travesty Hotel, I sauntered over to the icy receptionist, and offered a cordial greeting. Upon requesting to be accommodated for three nights I was told that all bookings were arranged via the internet, and the deadpan figure lifted a limp wrist, and gracelessly indicated a computer placed strategically near the door. Avanti. Of course, it wasn't working. The fiendish nature of the blessed machine meant that the problem was not apparent until you had filled in the Sudoku of questions and details required. The screen advocated patience, as the circle with the arrow spun, on and on, indeed promising, and failing to deliver some sort of progress. Two minutes maximum wait, and counting. Alas, no twenty minutes later, I returned to Dead Pan at reception. No, no. NO. He couldn't help. I would have to phone Travesty Central Bookings, I actually had a quick peek behind him to see if he was virtual reality—a cardboard cut-out of some sort. I could not trace a spark of humanity in the flat face.

Bookings confirmed I was standing in Travesty Central, and had inputted detailed answers to impertinent and, to my mind, unnecessary questions. Also confirming there was a problem, and promptly deleted all details I had put in, and asked me all the questions I had previously answered, again. Finally, this culminated in a reservation number.

Armed with this number, I again approached Dead Pan and waited, grinding my molars while several customers checked out. He insisted they filled in an evaluation form. Very clever form – ten being excellent, and one being barely acceptable. In fact, that's not quite correct, 'poor' was anything from one to three, while half decent to excellent ranged from four to ten. This left the responses highly skewed in favour of the hotel.

Having arrived at the decision that I was not going to waste conversation with the man, I silently handed over a scrap of paper with my reservation number on it. Dead Pan asked me if I wished to check in. How I kept civil, is a measure of my self-control. Forty minutes had already expired in nothing else but my futile attempts to do just that. Time, it is worth mentioning, that I will not get back again. I inclined the head in a nod. Early check-in meant a £10 surcharge. It was noon after all. Cash. I am not certain, but I wouldn't be at all surprised if that money went straight into Dead Pan's hipper.

Dead Pan then insisted on upgrading my room. I smelt a large, extremely doubly incontinent rodent, and protested against an upgrade. To no avail. There were 281 rooms in the establishment, I was now officially in room 240. As he handed me the key, I stated slowly and clearly, though my teeth were gritted, that I was looking forward to completing my leaving evaluation.

Of the cheerie, trouble free spirit of Kirst that had blithely entered the Travesty earlier, there remained not a trace. Not a bluebird's feather.

The bumps and frenzied noises outside room 240 at 4.15 in the AM caused me to jack knife awake. It was then I discovered there was no phone in the room. Over the course of the next two hours I managed to establish there were only about ten drunken Irish lads on a stag night, not the battalion of Black Watch that I had imagined. How your mind plays tricks in the early hours. After the first hour, I did contemplate walking the mile and a half to the reception to complain, but no sooner had this thought fleeted past than 'Brendan' or 'Donal' began to try to restore some order. It just took an hour before peace reigned again.

Upon approaching Dead Pan later that morning for my breakfast voucher, he enquired, looking down the length of his extremely long nose, as to whether I had slept well. I was glad he had touched on the subject matter foremost in my mind, and was delighted to unload an edited summary of my early adventures. I also enquired whether security guards or night staff were employed in the hotel, or was that department controlled via the internet? Dead Pan was pleased to inform me that all corridors were patrolled every hour. Tosh. Blithering, blatant, stranger to the truth, that Dead Pan. Still, I didn't want to add indigestion to my lack of sleep, so I just asked him for the number to phone, from my own phone of course, to call, should any further rude breaches of etiquette occur.

Night two was disrupted by a touring Welsh student rugby team. Lord, those boys could drink. The phone number given by Dead Pan went unanswered. Oh it rang, and rang, just no one to answer it. Things settled about 5.30 in the AM - thanks to some unseen lad called Garth. May he be forever treasured.

Dead Pan's explanation regarding the lack of answering the phone? The night staff couldn't answer the phone, as they were too busy patrolling the corridors. Cheek, face and bare – arrange in a suitable order. I noticed at breakfast that the rugby lads, looking none to fresh, were wearing luminous green kilts, and sporting red dragon sporrans. The kilts matched their facial skin, and the dragons their eyes.

Night three, and calm reigned until 3 AM. Glaswegian hen night. Sha-rron and Na-a-tal-eee were the two noisiest, but the rest of the pack were not far behind. I suppose it was like a photo finish scenario, if you could have imagined such a thing for noise. Bless. The next morning they came down to breakfast looking like a bevvy of models. Of course, they hadn't slept at all. Off to the Metro Centre they went. I think for sheer stamina the Glasgow girls won hands down in the noise Olympics.

I slid my room card with the aid of a finger, across to Dead Pan. He had turned, and walked away, when I arrested his progress by asking for an evaluation form. None left. I said I would be delighted to wait until he had printed one off for me.

I know that that evaluation form has not seen the light of day from the moment my back was turned. Will I visit Newcastle again? Yes. I had a lovely time, in daylight hours, and the City and its citizens are truly lovely.

I suppose the moral of this ramble is never, ever, ever, attempt to book into a hotel with a snippy receptionist.

NAMING A CAT

Cats, as informed sources are aware, cannot be owned. From the tips of their whiskers to the end of the tails they swish, they exude independence. It is pure folly to expect gratitude for lavish provision of food and treats. It is their pleasure to bestow their presence around you.

This in and out haughty behaviour has always rankled with me. I do not warm to them. The entire feline breed are in my 'cannot be bothered with the merchants' category. Of course cats always know when you cannot abide them. This causes them to make a bee line for you. Just out of pure spite. Not enough to sit at your feet, dearie me no, that's not intrusive enough. They will not be content until they have all four paws on your lap, with their claws kneading your upper thighs. Their tail in the vertical, and their bum facing you.

The proud owner, or rather loving serf, sees nothing wrong with this behaviour on the part of trickie woo. Cats get away with this arrant rudeness purely because they have fooled us into thinking they cannot be trained. This I dispute. I believe they can be trained, and in fact they are intelligent enough to be trainers of humans. They have us hoodwinked.

An Informed Source, who is currently besotted with a black cat who has residency in a house across the road, waxes lyrical about this cat. Most beautiful beast, etc, etc. This cat comes bolting across the road every morning at the first sign of any activity, intent on taking advantage of Informed Source's good nature and victuals. For this cat's singular act of thieving Informed is inordinately pleased. Eh? I just don't get it. Get thee hence you robber would be my reaction. I care not one jot whether you have had your breakfast.

The robber is, like all her ilk, very territorial. There is a cat across the way that she simply cannot abide. I don't know what occurred in the dim and distant – perhaps the offending cat ate an icing rose from her first birthday cake. Who can tell? However, both are battle scarred but the robber seems to have come off better. Her ears are in a better state. This bit of extra information makes me suspect that beauty really is in the eyes of the beholder. A beautiful cat with lacey battle scarred ears? Mmmmh.

Informed stays with his brother. Two men rattling around a house. Informed seems to be a house proud type of cove, and was frequently 'tutting' about some gravel which kept appearing on the floor of the kitchen. In discussions the blame was put fairly and squarely on the footwear coming into the house. No doubt the gravel had come in the treads of the shoes. Logical. There was then a bit of a spat about whose shoes. Both Informed and brother denied being the culprit. Defending their positions stoutly.

Sometime later, when cat came in, a tinkling sound was heard on the laminate. It was the wretched cat who had been bringing in the gravel. The cat was promptly christened Culprit. But it was felt that the beast deserved a title, as befits her status. So the robber became General Culprit. I believe it masquerades as 'Molly' in her own house. There's a lot in a name.

KIND TAKEAWAY

Ordering anything is an art form – seemingly simple, but as usual extraordinarily complex once more than one individual is involved, particularly if accents are centre stage.

Menus are perused, chins rubbed, choices considered – blah, blah, blah. To those with set requirements all this contemplation is just 'show.' Particularly infuriatingly when the procrastinator has gone through the entire menu, reading about five words a minute, and then decides to order what he/she has ordered every single blessed time they have previously ordered. Enough to make you scream! The discussions on half rice, half chips and 'swapsies' and shares are organised. All very well and good, but when the takeaway is popular, and delivery within an hour, tempus fugit, or more colloquially, 'horse on.'

For this ramble I am concentrating on Chinese food. They're efficient to the nth degree, and the food is always up to expectation. One takeaway meal lasts me for two meals – significant portions. Economical and tasty for lazy days.

Owing to my penthouse being first floor, with a deliberately inactive front door bell (I'm town centre) I have often walked the three-hundred yards required to order in person and waited, educating myself on what was in vogue at the brewers convention according to the magazines, and perusing the National Geographics, or failing that keeping one eye on the fish in the tank and the other on the Inverness Courier.

However, recent European funding has spruced up Academy Street, and what with cranes, scaffolding, new pedestrian walkways and general inconvenience, one momentous night, I turned right on Church Street instead of left. Purely to avoid folk outside Spoon's – a fine line between friends and ne'er-do-wells, normally related to the amount of convivial drinks consumed.

I can only say the right turn, followed by another sharp right, was serendipitous. For the individual with enough for a takeaway, but little else, a cabaret was provided free of charge.

A lovely lady, battling with the vagaries of English in Highland wrestled, and was flailing, taking the orders. Both on phone and in person. I don't know Cantonese, but I picked up the gist that all was not well in the kitchen, far from.

Now this was a Friday evening, and when I entered, 'workies,' by which I mean hard working lads in high-vis vests in desperate need of a pint, had been diverted by well-meaning wives and partners into picking up (and paying for) 'orders.' I could tell those lads were becoming tense, I wouldn't put them down as 'slavering,' but I would put their mood down as 'tetchy.'

From what I could gather, Fiona had ordered in plenty of time, and Iain was to pick up aforementioned, at 6pm. This was 6.30pm. Half the order was on the desk. The other half wasn't. The half on the desk was getting cold. The other half still was.

The delivery driver was out delivering. The deliveries awaiting delivery were stacking up. The phone calls coming in appeared mainly to be people cancelling deliveries because they had expected delivery within the hour, and that hour had well gone.

The harassed delivery driver arrived. Grinding his molars – he was self-contained, but had obviously had abuse up to his hair line. He had trouble coming in, as he was carrying a considerable number of deliveries which the recipients had refused to take – on the grounds they hadn't ordered this and that. Also, it appears no one had ordered cold food.

The harassed lassie behind the counter was beginning to wilt even more, looking positively bedraggled. And, oh I did sympathise, but the way she tore into the delivery driver gave me an inkling into what was going wrong. The C word, namely communication. Not enough off, and in no way positive. The delivery man was proper Scottish Highland and ginger to boot, the steam coming out of his ears would have done the orders for dumplings for a fortnight. Not happy would be to put it succinctly.

In sheer desperation, something akin to panic, the counter lassie looked at me. Great I thought, I've been trying to get my order in for fifteen minutes, and while this is undoubtedly entertaining, my stomach is grumbling.

'You!' she said, 'What you like?'

Well I said, 'BBQ spar/' no. That was me cut off.

'I know you, nice lady, you stay round corner, take this!'

'But,' I said rather feebly, 'What about money? And what is it?'

'Just cooked, and free. You help me?' Her eyes looked as if they were melting. Tears were not far away. Beseeching. I don't have a heart of stone. What could I do? I went away, helping her out you understand, with two carrier bags chocka of delicious food. Apparently the chef, and most are notoriously mercurial, objected strongly to mountains of food returning like a boomerang to the shop.

I could see where she was coming from. Near riot conditions now existed in the shop, but she did have the counter between herself and the punters. If however, the backstage staff got on her case, she would be caught in a pincer movement, and survival would not have been possible. She would probably have spontaneously combusted. Nothing would have been left of this girl but ashes and a puddle of tears.

I have eaten like a Lord for two days. And all to help my fellow woman. Isn't it just lovely to be kind?

THE THREE AGNETAS

On reflection, I have not finished with the subject of ordering takeaways from the orient. This goes back sometime, at least twenty years, when Encore was masquerading as a nightclub of sorts, the name of which escapes me. This particular evening, the club was hosting an Abba appreciation night. Well, three Agneta's left from mine, wedges, flairs and wigs akimbo as we sashayed to the dancing. Brilliant night. Danced our cotton socks off, wedges notwithstanding. I'm going to call my two dancing compatriots Barbara, and why not?

Now, my Barbara, is straight as a die. The other ain't. The first inkling of trouble came with 'the other.' Start a fight in a paper bag she would. Anyhoo, turns out whoever she was attempting to separate from his partner was actually more interested in Barbara or self.

Barbara and self were completely oblivious, we were on the dance floor, looking for Fernando. I didn't realise anything was amiss until I had a pint poured over me by an irate female who accused me of diverting her man's attention. And no, he wasn't called Fernando. I pulled my curtain of lager fringe apart, looked at Barbara, and with one mind we said, Irn Bru. The 'other' was ginger at the time – fake of course, she was just trying to kid on she was blessed.

Barbara was attempting to placate the irate female, the bouncers were asking if I wanted to press charges – no. The wretch who had been so taken by our dancing and complete disinterest was getting what for from his date. Irn Bru was hiding behind us, outwith range of missiles, clutching our jackets. We had definitely out-stayed our welcome.

It was in silence we meandered outside, I could hear Barbara's teeth grinding – always a bad sign. My glasses were sticky, lager, filthy, and between trying to clean them and walk with the wedges which had suddenly turned into lead weights, we were going nowhere fast. Irn Bru, meantime was chirping like a budgie. Busy explaining herself – or attempting to. The Jury (me) and Judge (Barbara) listened, giving nothing away, but the air was heavy with our displeasure. She had been tried and found severely wanting. This was unfortunately a pattern with Irn Bru. The sight of a happy couple enjoying a night out, was anathema to her. A red rag to a bull. She just couldn't help herself, it was like a compulsion, she just had to 'get in aboot.' Her other favourite pastime was accosting random male passers-by, and asking them which of the three of us looked the youngest/was the best looking. Any self-respecting randomer always decided on either Barbara or self, having summed up the measure of Irn Bru as akin to a six foot wooden spoon.

Barbara decided to treat us all to a takeaway, which was very decent of her, and we wandered now with purpose to the not-so-distant purveyor of Asian cuisine. Barbara ordered, Irn Bru ordered, I ordered. Barbara and I repaired outside for a contemplative smoke. Irn Bru, being a compulsive non-smoker remained within the shop.

Time progressed, and the order duly arrived. Barbara questioned the bill. The irate customer service assistant (I believe that's the pc title, if not, forgive me), began to itemise the items, and painstakingly go through the order and the sums. Barbara objected to the sudden appearance of Chow Mein, remonstrating that this had not been ordered. The assistant was adamant it had been, and upon further questioning pointed a menacingly chubby finger in the direction of Irn Bru, Who had the grace to blush. She had added to the order, once we had vacated the shop, and had failed to mention this the entire time the cabaret of the dispute had taken place. Barbara questioned Irn Bru, who denied any knowledge of Chow Mein. Barbara paid up with a bad grace.

If the exit from the club had been quiet, this was as nothing as to the exit from the takeaway. I had never understood the phrase the 'thickness of silence' before. But, I can assure you, there are some silences you can cut with a butter knife, and this was one uninterrupted thick fog.

I have never set foot outside with Irn Bru from that day to this. Don't get me wrong, this was but a sample of carnage which followed this woman throughout her life. For all I know she's still at it. And fair play to her. But for me, that night, was the full stop, the last straw. Though perversely, my hair after the lager shampoo was in fantastic condition, but the wig was a goner. Always look on the bright side. I hear from Barbara various snippets of her progress through life, and while not wishing her any harm, my sympathies are always with the poor victims who get caught in the web of lightning that surrounds her.

CARING AND SHARING

The fashion for volunteering is waning. The vast majority of charity shops on the streets are manned by redoubtable women in their seventies. As they shuffle off there are precious few coming in to replace them. This is a puzzle to me. I think it is good to volunteer for a cause close to your heart. You provide as much or as little time as you can afford. The key is reliability.

Charities have been getting a bad press of late, and rightly so in some cases. The payments to directors and various shenanigans which have been highlighted have soured relations. It is often felt that the upkeep of offices based in London could be put to much better use. And why have head offices in London at all? Relocate. I am sure Redcar would be delighted to offer you premises at a very low price.

The proliferation of charities also mean that there is too much money spent on duplicating work. All keeping people gainfully employed, but rather going against the grain of the original idea of the charity surely. Why not amalgamate all the cancer charities into one charity for all the different types of cancer? The British Heart Foundation, The Lifeboat, short snappy titles that say exactly what the purpose is.

Caring and Sharing gets donations locally, and the proceeds are spent locally. Charity in this case beginning and ending at home. Rightfully in my view.

I am the muscle. By this I mean that I go around with Izzy and pick up donations. The work is varied, and the donations cover a wide variety of preloved items.

The bonus for me is that it's the only place in the world where a fifty-four year old can be called a 'lassie.' I am not in need of a knee or hip replacement. I am not retired. I can carry stuff. I don't want to steam clean, iron or wash items. I simply go out and about lugging stuff around.

A particularly hot day in June, in a flat that was three floors up, with no lift, Izzy was offered a huge sideboard. Which she accepted with alacrity. I had doubts as to whether I could carry the thing and also whether it would actually fit into the car, but Izzy knows the space to within a millimetre. We had to go back to the shop to empty previous pick-ups, as it was blatantly obvious that it would be a tight squeeze. We also picked up a tape measure.

I am going to gloss over the nightmare of getting the thing down the stairs. Then back up and down for drawers. The back of the estate car would not quite shut. So we had to use the tie rope. The passenger seat was flattened for the drawers. It was felt that the only manageable way for the return trip was for me to lie flat, one foot wrapped around the flattened seat, clutching the boot end of the sideboard. How we came to this realisation I do not know. All I can say is that I needed minimum persuasion. I must have been suffering from some sort of heat stroke.

Duly ensconced and the tie rope in place, we proceeded, slowly, to negotiate the drive down the hill. Thank the good Lord we were going down. The tie rope snapped, and the back door swung alarmingly open. My wee foot was firmly in place, and I was clutching the said sideboard like a goodun.

Izzy proceeded slowly. There was a half- hearted offer to pull over, but what would have been the point? We had no other rope. There was nowhere to pull over. I opened my eyes as we passed Farm and Household. Having established we were on the flat and had shuddered to a halt at lights. The driver and the passenger in the car immediately behind were chortling, and more worryingly videoing or taking pictures with their phones. I didn't even have the strength left to make any sort of gesture. The situation called for a response, but I was found wanting. We arrived at base and disgorged the thing. Apparently, there were a few scratches on the top of the unit. Now I bite my nails, but I feel it could have been my fingers embedded in the top that caused the damage. Anyway, the damage was sorted, the thing was sold, and to add insult to injury we delivered it to its new owner within the following fortnight. This time the rope held.

On a particularly icy day in December, we were called to pick up a three-seater and two recliners. It was beyond me how the furniture had got into the room. I think the house must have been built around it. This is where Izzy's experience is invaluable. She can sort out angles, and sideways up, shuffle base etc. The added complication to what was already complex was that the immediate environment was a sheet of ice. Solid and unrelenting. We had our wellies on, but the car on the way down felt as if it was running on skis. The wellie soles were of little of no use.

This is where my experience comes in useful. I decided to sub contract the entire operation to two passing gentlemen. And they accepted the commission. They thought we were a little lacking in the neuron department to have even considered the removal in the first place. We encouraged and cajoled from the side lines. Izzy instructing and directing. We had to make two trips. We left those two Christian souls like raggy dolls. The kindness of strangers. I do hope we didn't put them off any further acts of heroism.

I suppose what I am trying to say is that when you stroll along the charity shops, peering at what is on offer, have a thought for the sheer effort involved in filling the shop. The generosity of those who contribute, the work to get it into shop, then from car to shop to hangers to steaming to new owners. That's not including the cleaning of ceramics, glass, and jewellery. The storing of items which are not in season. The continual tidying up after customers. There's no shop in the world that wouldn't be tidy if it wasn't for customers. If there is a way of putting the hanger on facing the wrong way, that is the way the customer will choose. It's like the first rule of retail. All volunteers are priceless – there is even a note to that effect on the wall beside the till.

But you know, when the money raised is spent on a myriad of good causes, and the ripples of goodwill from all the effort filter back into the community it is worth it. No Head Offices in London. No extravagant jaunts. Money staying local. I would recommend the next time you have a clear out that it is Caring and Sharing, you call.

DANCING THE TANGO

Sant Agata, Sorrento. Beautiful Italian village. The hotel Isla and self had been booked into was great. Homely, previously stately, little paint and touch ups required. Family run. Relaxing. Just what we had ordered.

Isla runs 'Hair by Isla' in Nairn. A startlingly successful business entirely due to her skill, professionalism and kindness. A very amusing and entertaining lady who I am proud to call my friend. Another business plug, she's doing a book launch event for me once I've written the blessed thing.

The first couple of days as we poodled about, we were waved at, and 'hello's' were shouted. By day three, we had gone native. We wore our crumpled clothes with attitude, and had been assimilated, the near death incidents from charging vespas were dealt with by a shrug. An American tourist actually lost her voice by the third day, hoarse from shouting to Vespa drivers. She also must have packed an iron. Didn't blend in, that's what I'm getting at.

The organised tours were done as far as we were concerned by day three. Blistering heat, long drives, hairpin bends, irate beeping drivers, not relaxing. And the chitter chatter on the bus.

A dusty leaflet at reception advertised a trip to a lemon farm. We got reception to phone up, and were duly picked up by a handsome dusky young man, in short shorts and little else.

The sight of the trees, all on a slope, stretching down forever. The heat releasing the citrus smell, and it hung in the air, just wrapping around you. There was wooden scaffolding made from hazel and some metal walkways at the height of the trees, to enable the pickers to pick. Made you dizzy looking up. Those pickers earned their coin.

The family who leased the place had been there since Vesuvius erupted. Part of the barn used to be part of a monastic organisation, all nooks and crannies with haunches of ham drying from the ceiling.

Pigs and a cow were confined to a big barn, not allowed out. Seemingly the policy in Italy is to allocate areas exclusively for specific branches of farming. The Sorrento area has been assigned for lemons. It seems to work. The geography of each particular area influencing the crop or animal farmed. Quite sensible I suppose, but a poor craic for the beasts confined.

Later on in the week we adjourned to a restaurant, bar, come karaoke band carry on. It was a great night. Only slightly impaired by the owner suddenly appearing at my left elbow when I was washing my hands in the ladies. Gregori was a small man, barely reaching my shoulder, but appeared to have eight extremely busy arms. After jumping up from the sink when he appeared I naturally assumed I had made a mistake and gone into the gents. But no, as we wrestled to the door, it was definitely the ladies.

Isla was laughing fit to burst at the table, as we catapulted out of the ladies onto the floor of the restaurant. The regulars didn't bat an eyelid. Anyway, I do remember getting to the table and was just about to sit down when Gregori stopped the band, and announced the he, and this lady (me) were now going to dance the tango. Excuse me! Wild cheering followed this announcement, and the Japanese tourists switched on their cameras. I looked panic stricken, so Isla assured me later. I certainly felt extremely uncomfortable. I asked Isla, 'Can I dance the tango?' She quite correctly pointed out she didn't have a clue, it never having come up in conversation. Thankfully I had recently watched 'Scent of a woman,' and thought I could probably manage it. Gregori had rushed to a random table and returned with a bright pink carnation clamped between his teeth. The game was on. The band was tuned.

I was reliably informed that I danced my socks off, and somehow got that carnation transferred to behind my ear. We were a hit. There was no denying it. We had cornered the market for the entertainment of the evening. There were shouts of 'more!' I felt that it was best to leave our public while they still wanted more, rather than rely on the seam of luck that had sustained the dance. Gregori sent a couple of bottles of wine to the table, the rest of the crew at the table with us were holding their sides and wiping their eyes. I couldn't help but feel that the cries of 'more!' had come from them, with a view to getting even more mileage out of my misery.

The next night we returned to the same place. Gregori thought his Christmas had come early. That man was a danger. I looked into his face, and said that I had such good fun the previous that I wasn't returning home, but staying with him, forever. The look of fear on his coupon was sweet revenge. He tiptoed around to the kitchen and stayed there. We got a complimentary range of starters sent over. And there was much merriment as we all got up and hit the Karaoke. Isla got a hellish review. The locals put their fingers in their ears and shouted her off. Gregori eventually sussed I had no intention of doing anything other than going home at the end of my holiday. I managed quite a decent conversation with him in the end. Apparently his tactics normally work, and he ends up with a fling for a week.

As I pointed out to him, and he had to agree, I had flung him around the restaurant in the course of the tango. You don't mess with anyone in the Highlands who has been brought up with the strip the willow. That's a dance you know you've danced. All corsets need adjusting after a session of that. Good luck to him. But watch out in the ladies.

SCOTTISH JUSTICE

As a support worker you frequently have to support your client through the tortuous process of Scottish Criminal Justice. The Justice System at the moment is groaning under the strains of space policy – don't bother sentencing for less than three months, as we have closed as many of the prisons as we can, and filled the rest to the rafters.

So, there is pretty little chance of going to prison, and don't the feckless know it. I have had my fair share of being in the public gallery. In fact, one of the downsides to any work of this nature is that police cars will slow down as they pass you they recognise your coupon, and it isn't until they place you, and recognise you, that they continue on their way. Lovely.

One of my 24/7 clients, a woman in her late thirties, I will call her Nemesis, has hospitalised four carers. Yes, four. And yes, hospitalised. She has been to court at least four times, and each time is released with a final, final, warning.

Nemesis has been in care since she was seven. In that time, with care, she has learnt to smoke and become an alcoholic. She has not, however, learnt responsibility. Before the cut backs, she used to require two carers, 24/7. Now it is just one – and by all accounts her behaviour now is worse. As a carer you get @ £30 for a sleepover. You do not get an hourly rate after 10pm, when whoever assessed her care needs has decided she will be snoring away, getting her eight hours beauty fix.

I went through a period of working weekends with Nemesis. On her first shift she informed me that her previous carer had 'fallen down the stairs.' Pushed, my dears, pushed. The poor soul is still signed off. This gives you a glimmer into Nemesis's world. Note the memory of the incident, and the intent to inform me. Not a whit abashed by the thought of the poor carer.

Nemesis has a shedload of medication, which the carer administers. No training necessary. The medication is kept in a safe, as Nemesis would, and indeed has, necked a week's ration in one go. Again, lovely.

Nemesis's Psychiatric Nurse, Gormless, visits once a week for half an hour, and professes himself delighted with her progress. It is difficult for those of us dealing with her on a 24/7 basis to share this view.

Nemesis's boyfriend, Norman, visits often. Particularly at the weekend when he is permitted to sleep over. Between them their mental age is late teens. They go upstairs to play 'trains.' I'm delighted to be able to inform you that Nemesis is on contraception, though that too is controversial – liberal souls reckon everyone is entitled to a child, and this week Nemesis wishes to become a mother.

A misguided social work individual thought it would be a good idea for Nemesis to be given a kitten, as opposed to a baby. The kitten annoyed her one night, so she flung it at a wall.

The long, long days are generally spent watching Harry Hill's TV Burp. The level of attention required to focus on anything other than 'snippets' is entirely absent. All attempts at involvement in home baking fail. At drawing. At talking for any length of time. At cleaning or household tasks. Or walking. No interest – or a deliberate failure to engage in activities that can best be left to others to do? I mean, it is a rare person indeed that finds ironing therapeutic. Nemesis's daily allowance is handed over, and she hot foots it to the shop for her ciggies and wine. The carer trails along, wasting oxygen by recommending other purchases. Her big shop is done on the day her disability living allowance is paid. This is non-negotiable.

The booze run done, and homeward bound, the trick now is to ensure the wine is stashed before it can be funnelled. When the sun sinks the cajoling begins. Gormless has decreed that Nemesis can have a glass of wine of an evening – she has bought it after all, and who can argue about her right to enjoy a glass. Gormless is deaf to all queries about a glass turning into a bottle. He will also turn on a 20p piece and say Nemesis has no capacity for understanding certain things. I can assure you, she is fully aware of the difference between a glass and a bottle. Very much so.

Once the bottle has been tanned, Nemesis turns into a monstrous caricature of all your Halloween horrors. Oh, and she doesn't go to bed for 10pm, ever. In fact 10pm is normally the time she is incontinent, with projectile force, in front of you. Wear wipe clean shoes is my advice to anyone doing a 24/7 shift in the community. Lovely. On giving the night time medication, I notice the 'not to be taken with alcohol' in bold. I withhold the medication, and put a note in the communication book to that effect.

Next weekend at handover, my esteemed colleague attracted my attention to an irate note left by Gormless:

To all carers, Nemesis's medication must be given on time irrespective of whether she has had alcohol or not. Nemesis has a basic human right to take the decision to enjoy a glass of wine. Yours etc Gormless (CPN)

That I'm afraid was it for me. Do you think Gormless would be considered responsible at the fatal accident enquiry? Nemesis staggering up to bed with a litre of wine sloshing in her guts, falling on the stairs and breaking her neck – entirely due to the side-effects of the combination of alcohol and prescribed anti-psychotic medication. No? Neither did I.

However, in court later that year, in the public gallery with another client, it was no surprise to me to see Nemesis called. Apparently an esteemed colleague had poured Nemesis's wine down the sink, after she had had a glass, in an attempt to prevent her getting galloping drunk for the fifth night in a row. After half an hour watching Burp, after the 10pm watershed, with a huffy protruding lower lip, Nemesis had got up, stating she was going upstairs. On the way past Esteemed Colleague, Nemesis punched her in the nose, breaking it, and causing a crimson tide of spurting blood. Again, lovely.

Esteemed tottered to the bottom of the stairs, just in time to see Nemesis coming from the bathroom with a bloody forehead, grasping a shard of the mirror she had just head butted. Nemesis proceeded to place this shard to her throat, and threatened to kill herself.

Esteemed colleague replied in a manner I am not prepared to share with you, and immediately Nemesis dropped the shard and raced towards the carer intent on removing the carer's head from the neck on which it was minding its own business. Thankfully Esteemed managed to wrestle Nemesis to the ground, promptly pinned her down, and telephoned the police to get Nemesis lifted, involving statements etc, before presenting herself at A&E. A night filled with the worst sort of excitement I am sure you will agree.

The Care Office's response the next day was 'You should have given her the wine,' and 'Oh, you will have to go to the station to pick Nemesis up, the police are releasing her.' Esteemed duly presented at the station, and the custody officer was reluctant to release Nemesis into her care, given the picture of her two black eyes, and a rather snappy white sticky plaster over her nose, not to mention the matter of the assault charge. After consultation between Police and the Care Office, Nemesis was eventually handed over to Esteemed. Esteemed drove to the Office, asked Nemesis to wait a moment while she went in and proceeded to give a force ten Navarone communication to the manager, giving in her notice with immediate effect, and lambasted the lack of care for carer's. Esteemed returned to the car, and asked Nemesis to go into the office, before driving away, several cup sizes smaller in the chest, having released a load.

However, the above was filled in later, I am getting ahead of myself. In the court, as the sorry tale unfolded, guilt absolutely undisputed, Nemesis was given yet another final, final, final warning. Surprise, surprise. There is nothing between the community and Carstairs for individuals with mental health and/or learning disability issues. Nemesis continues in the community with 24/7 care. In her two bedroomed flat – one for her, one for her uneasy, frequently changing, carer. Chi-ching, chi-ching, chi-ching.

The next court case involved an altercation regarding a hot water bottle and a one armed man I shall call Murdoch. Murdoch, after a congenial afternoon had invited a couple of worthies to his home for a couple of snifters. The next morning he reported the theft of a hot water bottle. The defence was that the accused was under the impression that the h.w.b was a gift, as Murdoch couldn't use it. That was me for the next twenty minutes. Could Murdoch use a h.w.b? If he placed the bottle between his knees he could unscrew the top. But, and here's the nub, could you trust yourself to fill a h.w.b held between your knees from a kettle of boiling water? The h.w.b incident had ended up in assault of Murdoch, prior to him pressing charges for theft.

The next case was my clients. Five charges. Two were dropped before going in, on condition she plead guilty to the remaining three. Another date was set for background reports. Strange that. My client had six charges last week and four coming up for next week.

She spends longer in court than the judge. No doubt she's up there now, or awaiting transportation from the station.

Just another day for the court.

UNDERWEAR IS NOT EXCHANGEABLE

I won't bore you with my early morning routine, suffice it to say that we all go through roughly the same process. I meandered to my knicker drawer with a view to selecting the choice of the day. I follow the Henry Ford School of Marketing, any colour you like as long as it is black. However, and this is probably where I should have started, I looked askance at my depleted stock. Over the past few years, yes years, I have had to discard scanties for various reasons – elastic gone, quality shot, holes like lace, a sort of tie dyed sludgy grey look going on, etc, etc. In summary there was no question in my mind but that urgent investment in stock was required prior to winter's chilly onslaught.

Goodbye, old friends!!! I'm off to get new pals. With this mission in mind I walked purposefully to the High Street store synonymous with scanties. Of course the store is very fly, tucking the 'drawers' in a secluded corner next to all other manner of what-have-you's that nestle to the skin. This of course means that in order to reach the corner you have to zig zag between blouses, skirts, shoes etc which does cause delay. Thankfully there's not much 'gasp' merchandise, the store seems to have adopted a consistent vintage approach. I worked for the store way back in the day, and in fact went in the huff with them when they refused to give me time off for 'Live Aid.' Gosh, that wasn't yesterday. I never set foot in that shop for twenty years after my disciplinary for going to Live Aid. However, I did go back eventually, having realised that my continued absence from their tills had affected them not one jot, and was in fact affecting the quality of my mother's birthday and Christmas presents.

Having reached the lingerie, the explosion of scanties and bras appeared in profusion. A wild variety of colour, flowers, laces and flounces. Very pretty, but not so much when it came to the larger sizes that needed the underwire scaffolding. My mission was clear and focused. Thongs are out, not after three children and at my tender years. Every time I see thongs I get a flashback to that Stringfellow guy on a beach. His backside looked like the elephant in Jungle Book, rear view as they crashed through the undergrowth.

Anyway, without taking you on my journey any further, just take it as read I acquired the necessary. It had taken a lot longer than anticipated, but then nothing in life is simple.

When the assistant at the till informed me that 'Underwear is non-exchangeable,' I said, 'I'm delighted to hear that.' I mean it's a whole new dimension to lingerie shopping to even consider the possibility of exchanging. But someone, at some point, must have attempted to.

DANCE IN HEAVEN

Elvira is a community patient. Donald is her doting husband of sixty-five years. Ex- RAF Battle of Britain pilot, with a magnificent white handlebar moustache, tinged with nicotine for the last three inches of each 'bar.'

Their house is large, sprawling over the crest of a hill on many different levels. Each extension – built as necessary for whatever reason of the time, was done with healthy respect for the howling gales and heavy winter snow. Windows are small, misshapen and pre central heating. The roof tiles are mossy, and the main eaves look as if Van Gogh designed it at the height of his passions. A truly random house.

The room they live in is small and cluttered. The small windows are sooty, but offer glimpses of lochs stretched out like a daisy chain far, far below. Uncomfortably hot from the heat churned out from a wood burning stove. Elvira has shrunk to a small fairy like creature, swathed in blankets, cocooned in a large winged chesterfield. Donald chain-smokes rollies at a square leaf oak table. As he smokes, he rolls. It is fair to say the air stings.

The space above the stove is taken up – six feet by eight feet – by a full length oil painting of Elvira in evening dress. A pale pink, limp, rose corsage at her wrist. A gorgeous copper dress. Flowers in profusion in the garden background leading to a castle or some such stately pile. Her eyes are the only recognisable feature. Penetrating blue, shining through the painting and her blankets. Donald had the painting commissioned before they got married. It caused their first argument, it cost six months' salary, so they got married on 'tuppence ha'penny.'

Apparently their parties were legendary – especially the winter ones. Strip the willow along the road, everyone wearing wellies and sliding in the snow. Bouncing in and out of ditches. Three pipers present, on occasion even playing the same tune. Twirls, skills, frills, and kilts.

There is a picture of Donald on the dresser, in RAF uniform. Distinctly Donald. In some strange way he hasn't aged, apart from his silver locks and nicotine tash, which actually suits him better than the harsh black of his youth. Much more mellow. There is still the touch of the romantic in Donald. You get the distinct impression that for two pins he would be twirling his tash and clicking his heels, elbows out and escorting Elvira for a night on the town.

After the hellos and general chitty chat, we arrive at the reason for the visit. Elvira's left leg has an ulcer. Everyone and their aunts in the NHS have been out to see it – wound specialists, the lot. The prognosis is not good. Several doctors have recommended amputation as the reluctant solution. Elvira has listened intently to each recommendation and sweetly, firmly, refused to comply. She's old school and she drawls clearly and consistently that 'I intend to die with all my bits dear. Anyway, how will I dance in Heaven with only one leg?'

Her skin is so thin it is translucent. The leg itself, in keeping with the rest of Elvira, is painfully thin. The leg is slowly but surely 'switching itself off.' Elvira eats crumbs, her very, very limited energy requirements are outpacing the fuel she requires. Liquid supplements are prescribed, but a glance in the fridge is enough to establish that the entire consignment for the past fortnight has been singularly undisturbed. Elvira smiles sweetly and insists she drinks at least three a day. What can you do? You can hardly call her a liar, which in essence is what her statement deserves.

Donald is Elvira's carer, and guards her protectively. No man has ever had a commission that suits him more. All offers of taking Elvira into the local hospital to give Donald 'respite' are refused. With humour, politeness and a firmness that will not be denied. They are a couple so thoroughly at one with each other they can say more in a glance than many others can do in a fortnight of speech.

Elvira and Donald always seem delighted to see you. Their manners are of a bygone age, but they are essentially so self-contained and content in each other's company that they hardly notice your presence. It makes little or no impact, and why should it?

Two weeks later Elvira's leg became gangrenous, and she became unconscious. Donald signed the necessary and the leg was amputated. They both died within hours of each other the next day. Elvira first.

THE HAUGH BAR

Way back in the day, there was a bar in the Haugh which with a singular lack of imagination was called 'The Haugh Bar.' It was a bar for locals. Not many from outwith the parish strayed into its environs. It wasn't encouraged.

The seasons were closely followed by the worthies who drank there. I'm talking fishing and shooting seasons here, though the usual hoo-ha went on during the football or rugby season. The first day of the fishing season was a big event. A drammie of malt was poured into the river, and the tall, tall tales began. This catch and release carry on caused a lot of debate. It was felt the policy was fine up to a point. The point was this, you could not be guaranteed catching a second one. Might it not be better therefore to release the second one? This, an environmentalist argued, was no use. A man who was fishing for a salmon, wanted it fresh for the pot. Once a fish was caught, it would seem likely that the contented angler would horse on home.

The environmentalist was very much out of his depth. He had no idea of his audience. Half the fishermen were not fishing with a view to providing food for themselves. Indeed, they hotly contested that that would ruin their trade. They could not afford to eat the salmon they caught. These salmon were sold at the back door of hotels to feed the insatiable appetites of the tourists, and to provide hard earned for the worthies to exchange for the convivial drink of their choice. Debates of similar nature were conducted throughout the entire season. Pros and cons and rights and wrongs occasionally resulting in the more spirited settling the matter in the Pictish manner of a fisted blow, which usually terminated philosophical discussion for a whiley.

The domino team during the season was another hot bed for acrimony. The difficulty in getting eight sober people consistently on a Monday night to play in the league meant that you had to register at least fifteen. To play with an unregistered player could theoretically mean the other team could claim the game. Serious stuff indeed. There were at this time five domino leagues in Inverness. I know. Five leagues. When they say there is nothing to do in The Highlands they have got it so wrong.

The Haugh were languishing at the bottom, of the bottom league. A vigorous recruitment drive resulted in women being targeted – they were considered more likely to be sober on a Monday night. It was a desperate measure, taken purely as an extreme solution, in order to restore The Haugh to its rightful place at the top of the top. The older worthies were absolutely disgusted – women it was felt, had no business playing dominoes. It was first and foremost a man's game. They couldn't even hold their doms, not having hands like a haunch of beef. Fears were allayed when it was explained that only four women would ever be in the team at each match. Parity would be maintained. Women would not take over the beautiful game.

I was one of the women. We were trained up by Old Iain and Vision of Loveliness. Their methods were pretty brutal banter. You had to cast any female sensibilities out of the window, the verbal volleys left no room for manoeuvre. It became second nature to carve your fellow players mercilessly if they did something unforgivable, like for instance chapping when they could have played.

We started in aboot league five and rose straight to the top. Ah, that was a lovely league. Civilised. The intermission drinks and food were excellent quality. Usually soup and sandwiches left over from an earlier funeral. Classy is what I am getting at. Our victuals when we hosted were half hearted sausage rolls, which if we could get them cheap because they were near their sell by date, we most certainly did. The reason for this meteoric rise, apart from our brilliance, was the fact that we were playing against hotels that didn't have local support, or at best it was half hearted. They couldn't provide a sober, consistent team. Slam dunk.

As we progressed remorselessly through the leagues we were also trawling through some of the roughest bars in the town. The higher you went in the leagues, the rougher the pubs. It was half way through the second league that Vision got his nickname. He was my doubles partner and he was absolutely shameless in flirting with the opposition females. In fact our chief tactic was to put Vision and self against two women. He would be straight in there, claiming he couldn't concentrate with such a 'vision of loveliness' across the table. He would also enquire as to where they had purchased their 'beautifully becoming' blouses/jumpers. Age was no barrier; he did this consistently every match he played, whether the woman was eighteen or eighty-one. And we all melted. A lovely man. Full of nonsense, but charming, and to those of us in the know, absolutely besotted with his wife.

We tried to claim the game in the downstairs Market Bar, on the grounds that there was a fight going on around the game. This was disallowed, as it was claimed this was normal. The Keg turned up dressed in drag. The back bar of the Gellions used to crowd round the table, you could practically feel their breath on the back of your neck. We were told to wear tight tops, and it was suggested that a touch of cleavage would work in our favour. Shameless tactics.

Anyway, I am getting carried away. This blether was supposed to be about the first day of the fishing. As usual, the place was stowed to the rafters on this most auspicious of all days. One of the local worthies came in and you couldn't help but notice a wriggling bag accompanied him. Upon enquiry this turned out to be a ferret. Nancy her name was. They had been out catching rabbits, which had been sold, and Nancy's owner had built up a thirst which he intended to address urgently.

Even The Haugh had a line. It was felt that a ferret in a bag was a step too far – not fair on the beast. The worthie refused to leave Nancy outside, on the grounds that she was a valuable beast, and he was convinced that someone would steal her. Anyway, the long and the short of the whole debate was that it was decided that the ferret would be released on the pool table, Nancy could rummage around the pockets and amuse herself.

Well the worthie's one drink turned into three or four, and we had all forgotten about Nancy. She had given us entertainment and a talking point, and it was pretty funny seeing her head pop up in various pockets. That's the thing with novelty entertainments, they soon lose their appeal.

A couple of lads from Canada who were backpacking around the Highlands came in. One ordered a couple of beers, the other went over to rack up the pool table. Not one man jack said a word. A hush fell on the hostelry. As the balls were getting racked, the lad at the table saw Nancy pop her head up from the top right corner. Nancy saw him, and disappeared. The lad shook his head, disbelieving the evidence of his own eyes. He looked at the bar, everyone was looking at him. No one indicated there was anything unusual which had taken place. The second lad sauntered over with the pints. He of course had had his back to the pool table so was oblivious to the drama unfolding. It was while the boys were tossing for who was going to kick off that Nancy appeared again, middle right pocket this time. The poor boys, they looked at Nancy, at each other, and finally at the locals. They retreated from the bar in haste, and Nancy's worthie snaffled their pints. It was felt that Nancy was indeed a valuable beast.

FAITH HOPE AND CHARITY

The bluebirds were tweeting round my head. The air was crisp. The sky was blue. The river was a ribbon of teal. In short, all was 'tickety boo.' The river bank was lovely, a carpet of white. Peace and calm reigned supreme, and all was right and righteous.

I studied 'Faith, Hope and Charity' on the go by. Highland Councils way of cheering us all up. Removing chicken wire dolphins with flowers and a half - hearted ivy was a good move. But in the worst economic crisis since the roaring 20's, and £60 on the spot fines for throwing ciggie butts, three transvestites in the wrong place is not going to do it. Hope is in the correct place, but they managed to swap Charity for Faith. One out of three correct is a fail in my book, but given the vast fortune spent on relocating the three trannies I am not surprised we are all keeping mum. The girls are a minimum size eighteen. Hefty is the word. Proper West Coasters. Strangers to salad. Chastity is not a bonnie haddock. She also looks as if she wouldn't give a sweet hello to a Big Issue seller, never mind buy a mag. Severe. Faith looks OK. Very demure. Perhaps they ordered a 'set' and got it wrong, paid less to get a slight 'second' production – Charity would be better in Faith's body. Hope? She looks as if she is spoiling for a fight, a right snippety looking bint.

Their previous residence had been on top of a building – out of sight and out of mind. I think our city fathers had the right idea.

WHERE ARE THE ARTHUR WILSONS?

I recently purchased a box set of Dad's Army, and was delighted afresh with their carry on. I had forgotten their flair for life, in one word 'exuberance.' I had also forgotten the charisma and general loveliness of Arthur Wilson. Well might Mavis cling to him like ivy, he's the stuff that dreams are made of. Mannerly, gentleman like, quiet spoken, and every word worth listening to. And when the chips were down, he battered the baddies. Lovely, lovely man.

Mind you, Godfrey, with his sisters controlling his life, his conshie point of view, and his distinguished Medal, would be right up there with Sergeant Wilson, apart from the fact he did have his two formidable sisters, and he was off to the toilet every two minutes.

Now, back to the title, where are the Arthur Wilson's? Where has this type disappeared to? Has feminism killed him off? Probably. I like a man to hold a door open, with his hand on the small of your back. I am well aware I can open a door, and though myopic, I can steer myself safely through the door frame. This is not the point. Someone, maybe even me if I am with a woman, will reach the door first.

I actually feel sorry for males – they cannot do wrong for doing right. To hold a door open for a woman can result in a blistering display of outraged feminism. Go through quickly, if you are in the slightest doubt as to whether you are in the presence of a militant, perhaps the door slamming in her face will cause her to reconsider.

Opening a door for someone you are with whether you are male or female, or in the company of another male or female is surely dependent on who reaches the blessed obstacle first. I don't expect or anticipate a blistering attack if I hold the door open for a feminine friend, I don't expect her to think anything of it, other than I have prevented facial injury, and am there purely to get us both through the door in the minimum time with the minimum effort. I don't expect her to feel that I imagine that she is incapable of holding a door open. If any female feels like that, it is her beholden duty to ensure she reaches the obstacle/door first. That prevents rudeness and ill will, and will enlarge her circle of friends immeasurably.

I like a man to pay for the meal. This going Dutch business should have remained in Holland where it seemingly started. The fact you feel compelled to join in this nonsense and offer to go halves is ridiculous. Men generally still earn more money than women. Women are generally entertaining. The price for our company should be at the very least that we are fed and watered. If our company is not entertaining, we will not be invited out for a rematch. This keeps us women on our toes.

And while I'm on this ramble, this Ms business is going a little too far. I know, I know, Mr gives no indication of whether a man is single or married, and why shouldn't women hide under the same umbrella of ignorance? Let's not advertise our availability, or otherwise. I get it. I just don't agree with it. Too far a step.

Of course, if both of you are working full time, the chores in the home should be shared. That goes without saying. But chores are chores, probably the word originates from the same root word as bores? I don't know. Someone with a classical education in Latin and or Greek could maybe enlighten us. I know couples who have a rota for chores. I would suggest this should get rolled up in a ball and thrown over the shoulder of your choice. Take this sort of thing to its logical conclusion. When you need the moss taken off the roof tiles, are you going to have a demarcation line on the roof? The female and the male halves. Call a man in? Are there any female roofers?

If the homestead is on fire, and you are at your window awaiting the hero up the ladder to rescue you, would you be happy if the hero was 5'4", irrespective of gender? I would be wanting someone who was at least broad of shoulder and strong in frame. I am a not inconsiderable weight. The number of females, other than your shot putters, who would fit my bill as an adequate fire fighter are few. How many female coal miners were there? Surely we can agree that there are differences in physical attributes between the genders. And if we can agree on that, we should divvy up tasks according to ability.

Of course anyone over the age of seven can do dishes, with a stool. If you do the cooking, and you have no dishwasher, then someone has to clean the plates. Unless you fancy eating off paper for the rest of your life. The number of labour saving appliances to reduce the monotony of household tasks has grown apace. But like the technology of email, mobiles etc have also introduced unreasonable expectations. Everything does not have to be done immediately. If it is a nice day, and the sun is shining bright, do not let the house bully you.

Leave it without a backward glance, and head off for an adventure – a walk, a catch up with folks you have missed, anything but housework. That house will be there long after you have gone. I am intending to have a plaque made for outside my house 'Kirsteen M Murray lived here from xxxx to xxxx, and enjoyed herself. Tidiness and neatness in the house was not her priority, nor what she measured her life by. She had family and friends and made them her priority. Think on.'

All I know is that in days of old, men used to disappear for years at a time, fighting in wars, pillaging or fishing, or what have you. Women managed everything very well, without any fuss. Of course when the conquering hero arrived home a welcome and a fluttering of females attended to his every whim. But this didn't last long. They cleared off again. Men would have been absolutely appalled to consider that they were not running the show. Women managed, in an undercover manner. The family unit in any fishing family was surely a matriarchal one.

When women demanded the same money for doing the same job that was purely and simply fair and equitable. But women live longer, yet we retired sooner. Now the retirement age has gone up for both genders. Women are asking, nay demanding, backdated payments. Men are not. Why not? We seem to be asking for our cake and eating slices of theirs. If there are no differences between the genders, and we maintain that stance, then there should be parity. But they should still open doors, and pay for meals!!!!! I know, I know, men just can't win.

RUDENESS

This is a big bugbear with me. There are lots of forms of rudeness. Being late is a big one – what you are saying by being late is that your time is more important than the time of the person waiting for you. To be consistently late, is therefore, to be consistently rude. I now make appointments with persistent offenders deliberately early. If I wish to meet them at 2pm, I make the appointment for 1.30.

Even worse that persistent lateness is those who fail to turn up at all. With no text or communication to the effect that their plans have changed. Now life can and does take twists and turns. I am not maintaining that all appointments can be met, you could have been slapped across the face with a wet haddock for instance, or stung by an insect of some kind, events which have taken your breath away, and leaves you too weak to face the meeting. I contend that in that instance, the only way to avoid rudeness is to inform and communicate to the other half of the sketch your inability to meet. This then leaves the other half to make alternate plans. All very civilised.

There are also 'bolters,' people you are out with who will disappear, normally before it's their round. The first couple of times, until this routine has occurred so frequently as to become the norm, there is genuine consternation. Where is so and so? Is she alright? Has she been abducted by aliens? Has that sleazy merchant gone out with her? A hue and cry occurs. 'Man down!' Phoning mobile produces no response. The bolter will be incommunicado until the following day at the earliest. Rude.

Another form of rudeness involves the 'scanner.' These lads/lassies will be scanning the immediate area, clocking every man/woman past puberty. Their ability to register the likely options or possibilities from a fleeting, raking, glance defies logical analysis. The ability to discern from a split second appraisal marital status, likelihood of wandering, and probably to the nearest penny what is in the wallet is nothing short of miraculous. This shifty eye scanning behaviour, always looking past you rather than at you, leaves the person opposite the scanner feeling underrated. Used until a likely lad/lassie approaches then you are dismissed, without a reference. Again, rude.

Then there are those merchants who use the f word every breath they take. It is so commonplace for them to do so that they appear genuinely unaware of it. Inevitably they talk at a high volume, and rather hog the limelight. As their stories, however amusing, are marred by the foul flow of filth coming from their mouths, they are not worth listening to. But, you are forced to listen, because you have gone out without ear protectors. And even more annoyingly you can't enjoy the conversation of the person you are out with, who is genuinely worth listening to. 'Is this a case of undiagnosed Tourette's?' I hear the Christian souls out there asking. Possibly, but unlikely. If so, there are a large number of those with undiagnosed Tourette's, perhaps someone could look into this matter, and place the findings before the populace. Maybe an on-the-spot fine system could be put in place. After all, you discard a ciggie in the street and there is the risk of being stung for £60. I would argue that there is more air pollution in the foul rantings of the uninteresting than there is from a whiff of woodbine.

VISITING A PSYCHIATRIST

There is a woman of this parish that has a son who was effervescent. Too bubbly by half. Couldn't be contained. Wandered like a meteor through his teens, attracted to trouble and fun like a daisy follows the sun. Life could never be too noisy and busy, a force of nature with more friends than foes, but indeed armies of both.

On this auspicious day, Effervescent had been told to be back from school at 5pm, a trip to Rollerbowl had been organised. At 3pm the phone rang, right in the middle of pancake making. Sergeant Macleod was on the phone. Effervescent was running along the roof of an established town centre store. Drunk as only a fourteen year old can be on Buckfast. Roads were closed. Town centre was stuck. Bridges were out of action. Police budget was getting stretched. A car was being sent for Mammy. In fact was purring outside, blues flashing.

Mammy got in car, still in apron, and was escorted to Macleod, who expressed his warm pleasure in her arrival. Chaos in the very stationary nature of the town's cars. A man with a loudhailer was attempting to speak Effervescent down from the roof. Macleod inclined his head towards loudhailer – 'he's trained,' he said. That was all Mammy needed to know as she exchanged a significant glance with Macleod. There is nothing so scary as someone who is 'trained,' but unfamiliar with background. Treat the patient, not the diagnosis. Macleod and Mammy knew Effervescent. This town would be blocked for a while.

A bevvy of substantial policemen hovering around, in a huddle, much like emperor penguins in the height of the inclement polar winter. Their mutterings were along the lines of the pay and conditions were not enough to induce any of them to venture onto the roof. They also knew Effervescent. Should we call a tightrope walker? Who is trained for avoiding missiles at two storeys up on the top of the slopey roof?

Macleod obtained loud hailer and gave it to Mammy. She of course had no training in this line, but she knew Effervescent. 'Get down off that roof right now!' she bellowed. 'I'm black affronted!!!' A fine pair of lungs. 'Macleod says there will be no charges, if you come down right now.' Effervescent came down. Mammy asked Macleod if herself and Effervescent could get a police taxi home. The answer was no. Mammy had been just a little optimistic. Slow plod home.

Macleod of course was up to his oxters in traffic control, dealing with irate delivery drivers and other petty matters. His abiding thought was that he had avoided the paperwork resulting from a fatal accident, and the even greater hassle involved in the ever spiralling police budget overspend. Everything at the end of the day is relative.

Mammy however was on a slow burn. Effervescent at fourteen was like a bothy cat with a firecracker tied to his tail. Enough was surely enough, could the lad be assessed by a psychiatrist? The police were very supportive. As was the GP. Everyone agreed – except Effervescent and the Psychiatric services.

In the meantime, as Mammy waited for an appointment, she bought Effervescent a book on Psychology. Effervescent was a bright lad, and it was felt in her naivety that if he got some insight into his behaviour that he would take steps to address the more outrageous aspects of his anti-social behaviour. Mammy was a poor deluded fool.

Effervescent inhaled the book in three hours and tossed it over his shoulders. He played her like a fish. Mammy was none the wiser he had assimilated the information, worse than that he had fully absorbed the gist, and could have probably written a treatise on how to continue.

The day of the appointment, months later, dawned clear and bright. This was in direct contrast to the dark clouds gathering in the house. Effervescent was not for going. Mammy was determined. Heads were, not literally, being butted. Carnage was avoided, bribery was used. And both attended like raggy dolls. The atmosphere in the waiting room was tense. Both noses were so far up in the air that there were parallel furrows in the roof.

In went Mammy and Effervescent. The psychiatrist was unaware of the two worthies she had in front of her. She admitted she had not read the referral, being of the mind that she could pick up more information by going in blind. A little arrogant perhaps? Another example of training. Dangerous thing, training.

Well she asked Mammy if she could call her 'Mother.' Mammy replied in the negative. This was not unreasonable. The age gap between them meant that

Mammy was much more likely to be Psychiatrists daughter. Besides, whether rightly or wrongly, Mammy felt that anyone who called her Mother should have been her own flesh and blood, not some unknown randomer.

Attention turned to Effervescent. 'Why do you think you are here?' Well if she did.

Effervescent looked her straight in the eye and said 'My mother clever batters me.' Psych asked for clarification, sharpening her pencil preparatory to making notes. Effervescent said it was clever battering, because his handsome face was never touched. It was all on the torso.

Mammy, by her own admission, lost what little patience the day had left her with. In a flurry of action, elbows being dominant, she launched herself at Effervescent. In a feverish battle, Effervescent's t-shirt was ripped in half and left in rags on the floor. Effervescent's alabaster torso was revealed in all its glory. Not a mark. Not a bruise. Not a scar. Nothing.

Well, when I say nothing, Effervescent was sitting there with a grin like a Cheshire Cat. Delighted with himself. If he had been a cat, he would have been taking a lazy paw to his whiskers, to brush off the last of the cream.

The psychiatrist meantime, had broken the pencil tip. The only physical damage during the duration of the appointment being the tip of the unfortunate pencil, and the t-shirt.

The appointment with Effervescent was suspended. He was removed by a very supportive staff member, and taken for some sasparilly.

Mammy was detained in the Psychiatrists presence. There were talks of assault charges. Psychiatrist was at a loss. Mammy could not get the point across, that there was not a mark on Effervescent. The Psychiatrists pencil had been re-sharpened and was whizzing across the pages. And pages. Effervescent was asked if he would like to press charges. After considered thought, he thought not.

Effervescent and Mammy left the clinic in silence, which was broken after a hundred yards by Effervescent saying 'you should never have given me that book on psychology.'

In the fullness of time the report came through from the clinic. Effervescent was absolutely within normal parameters, and dismissed without a stain or slur on his character. Mammy on the other hand was recommended to attend an intensive course on anger management, which she declined to do, on the grounds that even the thought of going on an anger management course made her angry.

The rights and the wrongs and the pros and the cons. I suppose if there is any point to this ramble at all, it is beware of training.

REALLY? SPORTY?

Why on earth is it considered acceptable for people who are obviously strangers to a gym to go around with sporting gear on? Is this secretly a wish fulfilment exercise on the part of those who wear an XXXXL sports top? Is this supposed to suggest that they are scurrying along on the way to a gym? Or on their way back?

Is it worn as a mark of belonging to a particular group or clan? Usually some football tribe. If so why the need? Are you looking for affirmation from other clan members, or other rival clan members? Is it a red rag to a bull? Are you in fact enticing some sort of reaction, either favourable or not.

Perfectly acceptable if attending a sporting event to wear the colours as it were. But out with the arena, I would suggest, no.

Same with trainers. Shapeless things. Comfort without style. I know there's a huge monetary industry supporting trainers and the wearing of them. But they generally soak sweat, that's what they are designed to do as you are working out. Teenage boys' trainers – yugh. But at least they are, or should be, participating in some sort of activity that involves the requirement for fast moving footwear. Something that is easy to wipe the mud off, and that a spin in the washing machine will not seriously impair. I can't help feeling that the exorbitant price of the more expensive trainers is purely to pay for the huge advertising budget. The difference between buying a sweatshirt with say two stripes, and one with say three, is huge. The quality may be arguably different, which means the quality can also be arguably the same. It only takes one person every hundred yards or so to say 'Emperor's clothes!' it is a con.

If everyone who wore sporting clothes had to attend the gym or prove some sort of exercise regime, the sporting clothing industry would be finished. In fairness, you can generally tell if someone exercises regularly. The results show. You are extremely unlikely to come across a flabby rugby player. Or a marathon runner with a veranda stomach.

The sumo wrestlers are active, and fit. And large. It doesn't mean that the measures that are currently used to indicate obesity are to be followed slavishly. Indeed they throw a myriad of discrepancies about – most if not all professional rugby players are considered obese.

But, for the vast majority of us, let's be honest, we cannot all have 'heavy bones' and an 'underactive thyroid gland.' We just latch onto these. We all eat too much, and do not exercise enough, or indeed at all.

CUSTOMERS

For anyone who has worked in a shop it will come as no surprise to learn that customers are not always right. I have sold everything from paper over the phone to clothes, with bags, purses, crystals, Buddhas and any amount of tat in-between.

Clothes-selling is the most problematic. I would go as far as to say a significant proportion of the population do not know what to wear. We all have lumps and bumps, and please pick something that hides the worst of the outline. Emphasise certain bumps of course, if that is what you are after.

I was walking behind a young woman today, and I could see her knickers (red) through the leggings that were fully extended around her curvy backside. I found myself thinking of the strain imposed on these leggings. My admiration for the elastic properties of the fabric went up a notch.

Some folk are sizeist. This is obviously a new word, as my laptop has underlined it in red. Let me explain. There are some people who will not buy a medium or large size. They firmly maintain they have always been a small. This is sheer nonsense. Sizes are not universal throughout the clothing industry. I am a twelve in one store, and fourteen in others. I have a top in a twelve that is larger than one of my XL tops. There is no rhyme or reason to sizing.

Don't get me started on Nepalese sizing. Their S sizes would have fitted me comfortably when I was seven. Go XL, my friend. I purchased a leather jacket in

Amsterdam that fits me like a glove. XXXL it is. I know! The Turkish man I purchased it from told me it made me look taller and slimmer. Utter nonsense. But I paid up without a murmur.

Americans, now that's a chubby race, generally. They do believe in covering their skeletons with an extra layer or so. And are generally addicted to wearing shorts all year round, just to add to the look of the thing. Their sizing goes way off the scale. I believe that those people you hear off now and again that remain in bed for years, doing nothing but eating and drinking purchase their clothing from American catalogues targeting those with girth.

There are also those that are vertically challenged. You know who you are, Rosie. I must admit there are disadvantages to being just over the five foot. Not least of which is the ability to get lost in a store, hidden by the clothes stands. Maxi's are generally out. Unless you develop the skill of hemming, once you have taken the foot or so off the original. However, you can generally get around that lack of inches by wearing frightfully high heels. It is not fair to ask your more blessed pals to go around in flatties, just to make you feel more comfortable. Though if going out with someone who is smaller than you, it is a good idea to wear flat shoes. Prevents looking down your nose at them all the time, and avoids a nasty crick in the neck from developing.

The worst clothing customers are ditherers. They will dither and dither. Generally they are not allowed out by themselves, and are attached to another, normally bored person, who they will constantly ask advice from. Before asking you, the person who is supposed to know the clothing available from the shop. Some clothes look poor on the hanger and great on. Take advice of the person selling. Obviously not to be done if the person who is selling the clothes looks as if they are incapable of buttoning their own outfits. If you don't like what he/she is wearing then go elsewhere for advice.

Now when you sell clothes you develop a knack for knowing what size a person is. Akin to an undertaker I would imagine. There is something heroic about stopping a person clutching a mishmash of the wrong sized clothing from going anywhere near the changing room. You know the buttons just wouldn't be able to take the strain. And forget those poor souls who buy clothes too small, saying it will provide an incentive for slimming. Delusional. Buy what fits you, if your diet goes well you will have a baggy jumper. If your impetuous diet fails, you will have that jumper in your wardrobe, like a constant reminder of your weak will. Glaring at you reproachfully. Furious at you for consigning a jumper of such elegant design to a life that is hidden. Cinderella at least got out for one night and bagged a prince. But not the cruel thing you have done, bought something that you are unable to wear. It's a great good job that clothes do not have feelings.

I have had a loyal following of customers, who will literally follow me from shop to shop, and who place themselves entirely at my disposal. I literally dress them from the skin out. They go uncomplainingly to the changing room, and await my arrival with armfuls of what-have-you's. My living Barbies. They come out feeling and looking great. The problem then is, which outfit to choose, oh dear, back to dithering.

Another type of customer is the stalker. They will do everything but buy the item. Haunting the shop. Trying it on at least half a dozen times. Just not sure. This is generally the case if price is an issue. I have been a stalker. I am ashamed to confess I placed my outfit on a hanger that was displaying a size that was two sizes below what it should be. Needless to say anyone who was a twelve trying it on, was disgusted at the sloppy fit – thinking they had worn down to a shadowy size eight overnight. All the sixteens' had sold out (or so they thought). I picked up that frock in the sale for little over a song. More of a tune really. There is no trick too low for a customer to try. You must be up to them.

I had a stalker of a ring in the other day. The ring was £8.50. He tried on three trays worth of rings before he found one that fitted him. A sort of trio of skulls. A statement piece, what the statement was fails me. Anyway, after his third visit of the day, he decided he was going to purchase. There then ensued a pantomime as he searched every pocket he had. Turning himself literally inside out. I stood about fifteen minutes of this. He had gathered £8.30, and short of turning himself upside down and shaking, there was no way he was going to reach the magic number. I halted proceedings before he checked his socks and said I would put in the missing 20p out of my own money. Well worth it. He went away satisfied. And I was much better pleased with the view from the till. Anyhoo, the peace was shattered when ring man came back with his community worker, demanding a refund. The community worker did not say that I was a disgusting follower of mammon, and had taken wicked advantage of a vulnerable soul, but I was under no illusion that that is exactly what he was thinking. Maybe he should have had a better idea of sticking like glue to his charge, that's what I was thinking. I gave ring man £8.30. And then the community carer pointed to the sign on the tray. All rings £8.50. I explained that he had got this ring for £8.30 and I had contributed the shortfall to the till from my meagre resources. To no avail. Ring man was doing a very good impersonation of someone who wouldn't be able to melt butter. I handed over £8.50. See what I mean? Low, mean trick. I'm down 20p, and had my patience stretched to near breaking.

Now, if a customer asks me what I think, I tell them. I know the temptation must be that to get a sale you just say they look fantastic. This is incorrect. They will go home and someone will tell them they look not at all attractive. To keep repeat sales in the long run, you must be honest. Not brutally so, but never let anyone leave looking worse in their new gear than they did before they came in.

Rug and throw selling is very annoying. Customers will come in and open lots and lots. Those that bother to refold them, will not follow the folds in the throws. Dearie me no. Anything but. Still that's better than the merchants who seem to wrinkle stuff into a ball and throw it over their shoulder. Rude. They are the same folk that will put clothing back on the hanger the wrong way. Fifty per cent chance of getting it right/wrong, and they unerringly will get it wrong one hundred per cent.

Selling crystals. Now that's something. The customer will assume, wrongly, that you have an expertise in the uses each stone is best for. A PhD in curing everything from addiction to increasing health and longevity. No. If I had such a gift, would I really be working in a shop? Not me. I'd be off like a rocket.

Mind you, most customers are delightful. Really nice people. And very polite. I think that's why the rude customers stand out so much. They are so very much in the minority.

DRUNKEN DUNCAN

It was not until Duncan was seen with a raunchy glint in his eye that the search began in earnest for the supply, and supplier, of the alcohol.

The hunt did not take long. Duncan Macleod was grinning madly, drunk in charge of his wheelchair. Hindsight being a wonderful thing we all recollected that he had kept himself to himself for most of the day. Not unusual in itself – he was generally fairly independent, and though social, he sometimes has a retreat. His son John had visited him in the afternoon and was the chief supply suspect.

I generally find the best policy when confronting a drunk as a lord resident, whether in a wheelchair or not, is brutal honesty. 'Duncan, you are pickled!' 'I am that lass.' Was the affable response.

'Well, before we go any further, I'd like you to tell me where the voddie is. It's been a long shift, and I am not in the mood for hide and seek.'

'Hee, hee, hee. It's in the drawer with my 'drawers,' third one down.'

Two finger widths remained from a litre bottle. That was suspiciously easy. Drink per se is not banned from the Home. Many residents have a wee tipple last thing at night. Their bottles are in their rooms and they self-administer. Not a problem.

However, Duncan's more your 'get it down your neck merchants.' He has a long history of falls from wheelchair while pished, and an even longer history of alcohol abuse. His family have been consulted about bringing alcohol in, and the recommendation is that alcohol should be 'declared' at customs/office, and the drammies will be provided on request in manageable quantities. But daily and limits are not words Duncan wants to hear in relation to alcohol, and he has been aggressive in demanding more and more drammies when the rationing system has been in place.

Anyway, the shift ended in half an hour, and after handing over to the Night Nurse – Fortitude – I raced out the building without a backward glance. Job done.

Fortitude's report the next morning was nothing but a catalogue of woes – all majoring on Duncan. The reason the voddie had been so easy to confiscate was that Duncan, the fly fox, was preventing a more thorough search.

Duncan was buzzing for assistance around midnight. Blazing. Surrounded by cases of super lager. He had also been incontinent. That was the start of a fairly continual scenario. Refusal to go to bed, and assistance to change. Fall three resulted in a graze on the head, but Duncan had become disorientated and crawled under the bed. Refusing help, and hurling obscenities at staff. One got the definite impression that patience was wafer thin – the night staff were but pale shadows of their former selves. Duncan's son had been impossible to contact (with a view to establishing the exact amount of contraband delivered.) An impassioned plea from Fortitude for day staff to 'have a word' with John, rounded off the calamitous tale, sorry handover. On balance I thought John showed sterling good sense in avoiding all contact from the Home.

This is a classic example of mass confusion. John knew, without a shred of doubt, that his father was incapable of rationing his booze. He never had done and was not on any road leading to Damascus. John also knew that if he brought in hooch that it should be given to staff to ration. But Duncan has a right to his choices, and if he chooses to get blind drunk, then why not? The 'why not' is the risk he places himself at through his falls. Imagine the scenario should a fall have resulted in a fatal accident? Who would be at fault? Ultimately Duncan of course. But John would not have been blameless.

The only thing you can say with absolute certainty is that the Care Home would get it in the neck. Care Homes always do, you cannot do right for doing wrong.

BEARDS AND BOOBS

Now, without entering the befuddling issue of gender allegiance, alliance or affiliation, let me make it clear I'm simplifying for the purpose of this ramble to two gender types. Namely male and female. Based purely on equipment at the groin.

Now, boobs are assumed to be affiliated with females, and beards with men. So far, so good.

Now, bear with me, as you get older, the two genders seem to 'morph' together. Men acquire boobs and women beards.

I look at the assorted paraphernalia regarding hair and hair removal in my home. A considerable collection, all taking up valuable room required for other more useful things, like books, shoes and miscellaneous.

Regarding hair, I am a firm subscriber to the whole 'wash and go' philosophy. I resent the carry on that ensues after towel drying. I have had a hair dryer for four years. I bought it when I moved into my penthouse. I felt mature enough at fifty to handle the intricacies of a hairdryer. OH? I hear you ask, surely a hairdryer is a simple enough machine? And yes, I'm forced to agree, for the age seven plus, that's true. However, I was a victim of the 80's crimpers and toasters. My hair was electrocuted on a daily basis. So much so that I went for a number two at the age of . twenty-one, and was mortified that the wreckage on the floor was not considered suitable for human wigs. There was some talk of using it for replacing stuffing in horse hair cushions. Be that as it may, once it was off I couldn't have cared a jot.

The trigger to the brutal skinhead was that, two, **two**, consecutive hairdryers had literally gone on fire in the process of drying my frizz. Enough, I thought, enough. And of course, with a number two there was absolutely no need for a dryer. A quick look over your shoulder and the hair was dry.

Hair grows like grass in my case. Remember those dolls back in the day who had a 'hole' in the top of their head and you hauled it out to required length. Bit like that for me. And thick like thatch. I am also blessed with a double quiff which shames Oor Wullie. Great in the punk era, I didn't need gel.

Anyway, in maturity, with said hair having gone from chestnut to silver, I am now able to use a hairdryer as the manufacturer intended, without blowing it up or setting it on fire.

Where was I going with this? Oh yes, hair in general. Beards in particular. As a person fully identifying with the gender specification I was born with, namely female, I shave my arms and legs as per my cultural identity. That's it for me. No more and no less. I did pluck one hair from an eyebrow at the age of fourteen, and as I evicted the said hair, I thought, no, and chucked the tweezers. I do not criticise or condone avid pluckers, I just state firmly, it is not for me. If I develop a monobrow, the case may very well change. Never say never, and all that.

As regards hair in the crossed legs region – best left I say. We were encouraged as young women in the 80's to stand astride a mirror and get to know our vaginas. I'm afraid I always had better things to do. If you want an idea of vaginal discourse, pay hard cash to go to an evening of 'vaginal monologues.'

The aging process means everything goes south. Not arguing with gravity at all, but how come the hairs appear on your chinny chin chin? Where have they come from? Have they slipped from your forehead or rebelled against gravity? They really, really have to go. I'm not going around like Billy Goat Gruff for anyone. Cream. That's the thing. Use a cream. Remove that hair. Militant pubic consistency, curly wurly's that appear two inches overnight. That's where the battle lies. I'll keep you informed.

I've noticed this ramble has gone on like a mountain stream, and the subject of boobs has not really been addressed. I shall do so now. Boobs are lovely, useful, squishy and exciting. Many a different shape and form.

To the men who will get them I can only say this – you've spent your formative being nurtured by them, your teens onwards keeking at them, fair enough, you have now got what you wished for! Your very own. Enjoy.

SWAPPING HEADS

Science is great. There was according to the wireless today an attempt to transplant a head. Always difficult to get volunteers for that sort of experiment, I would imagine. However, some poor souls heading for execution, had been offered the choice of allowing experimentation, or dying. They had gone for the former. We are talking places here where life is cheap, and harsh. Presumably we in the 'developed' world are just observing with interest. There was not a mention of trying to halt the death penalty or any such thing. No the interest was concentrated on the science of the possibility of a head transplant.

I just cannot imagine what goes through anyone's head when they are talking about swapping heads, after all you are essentially swapping bodies. The other half of the coin. Or do you disregard the body that's rejected by the head you are hoping to save.

Did they meet beforehand? Did they think – oh that's great if this works, I will be six foot four inches and have a six pack, instead of five foot four inches round. Or perhaps, yikes, I will have to spend at least a year in the gym to get rid of the overhanging veranda, I want my six pack back, and this body has gone, gone, gone. Are you able to specify gender?

Imagine if, God forbid, you had been in a near fatal car crash. The only way to 'survive' was to have your head transplanted. You leave your memories as a forty year old man, and you 'wake up' as an eighteen year old lassie. How on earth would your children, wife, family and friends react to that? Far less yourself. It is surely the stuff of fiction.

If this becomes commonplace, then rich people will advertise for young fit bodies to put their aging heads on, in an attempt to prolong life and achieve a sort of immortality. The poor volunteer would be purely driven by economic considerations. It is all very well saying that morals and ethics would step in and prevent this out-and-out abuse. But according to reports, kidneys are already for sale. There is nothing in this world that cannot be exploited by humans. Ethics and morals do not 'put the hems on' exploitation – check your history, and you only have to go back a week at the most.

What happens if you end up with a fantastic new body? Are you going to look after it? Are you going to carry on with your previous lifestyle? Are you going to carry on smoking? Drinking? Slobbing around in front of the TV? You turn the body of Venus into a full moon. Can you sue the transplant team that performed the operation?

If your head is undamaged, and transplanted onto the healthy body of a person whose head has been irretrievably damaged, is the official owner, the 'head' or the 'body'? I mean neither can survive without the other. Where do the respective families stand? Does the owner of the head owe anything to the family of the owner of the body? If a DNA sample is required for paternity, does it come from the body? And is the head responsible, if paternity is proved, for upkeep of an infant?

What about skills and experience? I mean the head can be that of an executive. The body may have belonged to a professional ice skater. Muscle memory of ice skating could mean that the executive suddenly has the unforeseen ability to skate, presumably while taking notes and making decisions.

Could this be evolved in a truly monstrous true horror story, where a super hero is manufactured? Take a super intelligent scientist type, with a puny, withered body. And a super fit, athletic lad, with a very low IQ. Would pressure be on to transplant?

Imagine a misshapen body was transplanted on the head of a page three girl who continued post operatively to ply her trade? Would the body's family be entitled to sue? Or at least ask for a cut of earnings? Or would the page three girl sue the body's family for loss of earnings?

These questions used to be in the realm of fantasy, but no longer my friend. Scary stuff. I look at my own head and body, and think NO. I mean we can all imagine we would change this and that. But really? If you want to change something just do it. Go to the gym. Get the boob job. Gastric band. Whatever. But change the scars you have accumulated in order to achieve perfection? Whether you like it or not, your body is a road map of your life. Freud reckoned you owned your face when you were forty. I think that's sensible. Your laughter or frown lines are yours. Time has imprinted lines which can be read.

Looking at those who have eliminated lines by the use of Botox, etc in a quest to look younger. What they look like is odd. Peculiar. We are built to subliminally read lines in one another's faces like a book. When the lines are missing, this causes us to double take. Never mind the complete lack of emotion these robotic souls show.

I would on balance advocate leaving well alone. However tempting to look younger or smarter or just plain better. You are what you are — suck it up, Buttercup!

WORKMEN

Now this is tricky. The general breed of workmen, irrespective of trade, are more sensitive than your most capricious model. They are quick to take a perceived insult, and have a habit of taking umbrage at the most mundane of comments.

I want it clearly understood that I value and esteem all workmen who condescend, in their own good time to arrive and attend to the myriad tasks that await them in and around my homestead. No doubt they prioritise, but I have found that if you have any sort of pull at all with their better halves, you have a much better chance of getting any work done timeously.

Failing having a connection with their partners, you have to build up some connection with them. And they are generally men's men, who drink and play hard, inevitably in a particularly hostelry which they nest in all year round. They will do each other 'favours' in this nesting stock exchange, and beers are exchanged and a general feeling of bonhomie will pervade their charitable endeavours. Lots of back slapping and hand shaking. And of course nodding. A perfect understanding of what is required is pervading the hostelry. Translating this tremendous feeling of goodwill into actual action, that's where the problems occur.

Deals that are done at midnight on a Saturday night, may not be remembered the next day, never mind the day of promised fulfilment. This results in delays. Once delays occur, and the recipient of the 'favour,' who is awaiting the appearance of the elusive workman, is quite naturally umbraged.

This umbrage is to be avoided. Treat it like fishing. Patience my lovely is required. If you throw the rod in after failing to catch on the first throw, you will never catch the fish. And you are after a particularly arrogant brute – a large perch perhaps. One who dismisses all others in his field as somehow not quite up to speck. Nothing along those lines is stated as regards his 'mates,' but others are considered more than fair game. Those in his particular line are in for the most vitriolic outbursts.

There is also a pecking order (of course there is!) regarding the trades. Depending of course on which trade that supports your lifestyle. I have had cabbage ear listening to sparks who claim to be the crème de la crème, while the dual heating engineers have no doubt at all about their claim to wear the tiara. The joiners come in for a hard time. Inevitably they have cut the holes in the wrong place, or put the skirting boards in a bit premature – even if they carry the work out according to the time schedule agreed. Plumbers, well, everyone hangs around waiting for them. They have inevitably underestimated the trickiness of the job. It isn't until the bath is removed that some insurmountable problem regarding pipes means that the small shower you originally envisaged now has to have a base the length of the bath you removed. And a step up. And a commensurate increase in all manner of enclosing materials. The whole idea of redoing the bathroom in order to put a shower in, and gain space, has gone. Along with the bath. Nothing for it but to persevere. Stick to the plan like glue.

I have noticed that painters are considered pond life generally, I have even heard someone say 'if you can pee you can paint.' Though I must emphasise that my painter, Billy Shanks, is excellent. When he turns up. After he had his cataracts done. You do need to supply a pound and a half of cake, and his weight in biscuits, permanent tea on the go. But he is a lovely man to have about the house. Cheerie.

Now another thing to bear in mind is that in this most male of male worlds is that 'a mate is a mate.' Admirable no doubt, and indeed a very laudable sentiment. But a mate that is turning his weekend into four days, leaves only three for work. And perhaps he is not at his best on the first of the three days. And anticipating his forthcoming weekend on day three. This leaves the optimum time to 'get him' on day two. You see the peril you are in if you happen to be a lone female, with the dire need for instance a heating engineer, and who has been rash enough not to have befriended the wife of a half reliable member of that trade.

I listen askance to yarns of reliable workmen, who not only turn up on time, but will answer your queries left on their ansa within ten working days. They always seem to be on holiday. This live for today sentiment, spend what you have before looking for work for the morrow, doesn't go two ways. When they decide they will come around and see your 'job,' that's not to do the job. Dearie me, no. You poor, deluded fool. This is just an assessment. I have had workmen in, who at the end of the assessment will turn around and say, in complete sincerity, yes, I will do the job for you. It is then you realise that they are actually interviewing you! I know. And by this time you are so grateful for the fact that someone has actually responded, you humbly thank the man. Really!! It is only when he is out the door, and you are clearing up the considerable mountain of crumbs from the hastily purchased pastry's which you dived out to get from the Co-op, hoping it would be in time for the five minute warning he gave you before he descended, that you realise he has left without giving you a clue about the time frame of the job.

So what's the story? Patience my lovely. At the very least you should have the mobi number for co-ordinating the work. Accept the fact that you have to be there when the work is progressing. Just to make the tea etc, fatal to let them leave the premises for sustenance. Bars are too close. Work ethics weaken in the afternoon. It is not unusual for a working woman, who (stupidly) remained at work, to come home on a Friday to a pasting table, with a roll of paper, caked dry, and a little note beside the table. Just off for lunch. Back soon. That particular cove turned up the following Tuesday. Get where I am going with this?

Make sure your work is aware and flexible, a moment's notice maybe all you have, and then only because someone not as wise as you has somehow annoyed this delicate tradesman, and they have walked out on a job. If you have pressing business – a surgeon or some such merchant - sub-contract the tea making to a reliable female.

You will have to go laden to your abode with a knee buckling tray of pastry delights. Be on permanent call for tea. Get in another bag of sugar. This is not a time for stinting. With any luck the mugs of builder's tea, laced with varying degrees of sugar, supplemented heavily by the shop bought cakes, will give the workers a sugar rush, and it will translate into work. Above all it is crucial to have any work due for completion by 11am on Friday. Work ceases by 11am. I would go as far as to say any workman working after 11am on Friday is just masquerading as a professional.

I am giving you gold here. These top tips have been realised only with pain and endurance, and careful study. Forget all about women's lib etc. Transplant yourself back to the 1950's. This will not change until the number of females working as plumbers, joiners, sparks, painters, skimmers, skaters, and whatever increases. Face it. Go with this particular flow. Be as uptight and umbraged as you like AFTER the job is done.

RICHARD S MONTAGUE

The more discerning of you will have examined the cover of this book, or pamphlet, depending on how many of the rambles eventually make it into print. While you were rubbing your chin, and contemplating purchase, you might have been favourably impressed with the review by Richard S Montague. 'The best book I have read in twenty-five years.'

Who you may ask is this Richard fellow? What are his credentials as a critic? Is his opinion a significant contribution to literary review? All valid questions. Fellow Richard is a successful entrepreneur, who owns a business at the cutting edge of hippy chic. For those of you interested, the shop is Far Fetched, based in Drummond Street. Initially, I thought the name referred to something that was unbelievable – such as the astounding value for money, but the name is in fact directly linked to the distance travelled by Richard to India and Nepal, in order to purchase the items for sale. He's been doing this for thirty years, and clothing is ethically sourced from folk he has had a long relationship with, and made for Far Fetched with love. As it says on the tickets. All hunky dory.

So that's the shop plugged shamelessly, but I notice I haven't addressed the question of literary review. Richard, by his own admission, has not read a book for twenty-five years. Obviously, he has hovered in fear and trepidation, once he heard of my mission to write a book. In fact the begging and pleading to not be mentioned, has verged on the admirable on occasion. However, he is the only person I know who proudly states he has not read a book in twenty-five years. That's liquid gold, for the front cover. So I am taking wicked advantage of his curiosity, and sort of drip feeding him a few ramblings at a time. Baby steps you understand.

As to his claim that this is the best book he has read in twenty-five years. True. The fact that it is the only book he has read in twenty-five years, should be celebrated as a major achievement by myself. And in forcing him to read the rambles, I have broadened his outlook and enriched his life. He hasn't actually said that, in any way, but I am sure that is the position. That's my take on it anyway.